to teachers and parents

This is a LADYBIRD LEADER book, one of a series specially produced to meet the very real need for carefully planned *first information books* that instantly attract enquiring minds and stimulate reluctant readers.

The subject matter and vocabulary have been selected with expert assistance, and the brief and simple text is printed in large, clear type.

Children's questions are anticipated and facts presented in a logical sequence. Where possible, the books show what happened in the past and what is relevant today.

Special artwork has been commissioned to set a standard rarely seen in books for this reading age and at this price.

Full colour illustrations are on all 48 pages to give maximum impact and provide the extra enrichment that is the aim of all Ladybird Leaders.

The publishers wish to acknowledge the assistance of
Mr R J Wootton Ph D, Department of Zoology,
University College of Wales, in the preparation of this book.

A Ladybird Leader

the stream

by Harold Stanton
with illustrations by David Palmer
and photography by John Moyes

Ladybird Books Ltd Loughborough 1976

How streams begin

Damp air rises
from the land and sea.

When the damp air cools
it forms clouds, and rain falls.

The rain sinks into the land.

Where the water bubbles out
is called a spring.

Some streams begin
high in the mountains.
Here it is too cold for many plants
or animals to live.

The headstream

Bubbling and splashing
the stream rushes down the hillside.

The rushing water washes away
all the small stones and mud.
Only moss can grow on the rocks.

Beside the headstream

The rushing water carries along
small rocks and stones
as it carves a steep valley.

Only rough grass, heather
and a few stunted trees
manage to grow
on the windswept hillside.

The trout beck

Now the water flows a little slower.
The stream becomes wider
and shallower.

In sheltered places
water plants with narrow leaves
grow in the gravel.

Narrow leaves do not get pulled off
by the stream.

11

Fish

Few fish live in fast flowing water.
Trout like fast streams.
Another fish, the Miller's Thumb,
spends its life sheltering
in holes beneath stones.

The trout live on insects, beetles,
worms and smaller fish.

The Dipper

The dipper comes here for food.
He dips and bobs into the water
in search of insects and larvae.

Around the trout beck

In the small alder bushes
on the grassy banks are many birds.

They are looking for gnats
and other flying insects.

Water plantain grows at the edge
of the stream.

15

The minnow reach

As the stream gets slower mud settles
Many more plants now grow.
The plants must have strong roots
and stems.
Water Crowfoot and Water Buttercups
have deep roots.

Sticklebacks and minnows eat
the insects hiding among the plants.

In spring the male stickleback
builds a nest in which the female
lays her eggs.

Then he guards the nest
and fans a current of water
over the eggs until they hatch.

Insects

Many kinds of insects lay their eggs
in fresh water.
Some eggs hatch into larvae,
others into nymphs.

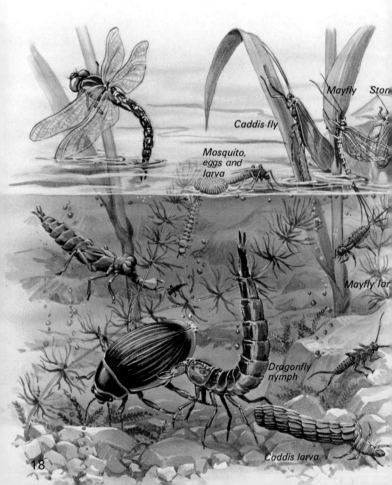

Mayfly   Ston

Caddis fly

Mosquito,
eggs and
larva

Mayfly lar

Dragonfly
nymph

Caddis larva

When it is a year old
the dragonfly nymph climbs
from the water.

When its skin splits
the adult dragonfly crawls out.

Dragonfly
emerging
from
nymph

Great
Diving Beetle

The larvae of gnats, caddis flies
and beetles form pupae
in which they change into adults.

Crayfish

Crayfish live under stones
and rocks.

They are related to lobsters
and shrimps found in the sea.

Crayfish grow to 10 cm long

The Kingfisher

The kingfisher waits on a branch
and dives into the water
to catch small fish.

Kingfishers nest in a deep hole
in the river bank.

Water power

Long ago many factories
used water power to drive machinery.

Water power is still used
to make electricity
in hydro electric power stations.

Grain

Flour

At one time millers used
the power of the water
to grind flour.

Beside the minnow reach

Water-loving trees like the willow trail their branches in the stream.

The roots stop the soft banks being washed away.

Among the leaves many insects live in the shelter of the branches.

The wood of the white willow tree is used for cricket bats.

Osiers are small willow trees.

The long thin branches are used for baskets.

The lowland reach

When the river reaches the flat land
it flows very slowly.

Gently the river winds its way
to the sea.

Gradually the river changes its course.

On the outside of each bend
the water wears the bank away.

On the inside of each bend
thick mud settles.

Following storms
the banks are worn away even faster.

If the surrounding land is flooded,
silt is left behind.

Gradually the valley becomes flatter
and flatter.

Many plants and animals
live in this part of the river.

The slow moving water
does not damage the plants
and roots are firmly held by the mud.

Arrowhead

Water Starwort

Bur-reed

Water Lily

Canadian Pondweed

Canadian Pondweed
grows under water.

It really is a Canadian plant
which is used in an aquarium.

When a piece breaks off,
it grows roots and is able to grow
into another plant.

The food chain

Insects need the plants for food
and shelter.

In turn the fish feed on the insects.

Larger fish and birds eat
the smaller fish.

Fish

Fish stay where it is easiest
for them to live.

In the slow moving river
they do not get washed downstream.

Perch

Roach

Carp

Dace

Gudgeon

Pike

Mammals

Otters hunt and play in the river.
They feed on fish, frogs
and small birds.

Like most water animals
they live in burrows
under the river bank.

The Water Vole is often called
the Water Rat although it is not a rat.

Coypu

Water Shrew

Water Voles

Coypus are American animals
which have escaped and live wild.

The river banks
in which they dig large holes
sometimes collapse.

Amphibians

Frogs and toads lay their spawn
in quiet pools.

Although thousands of eggs are laid,
few become frogs and toads,
because the tadpoles are eaten
by birds and fish.

Newts

Newts hide their eggs under leaves.

Their tadpoles grow
their front legs first.

Newts, toads and frogs
are called *amphibians,*
because they can live on land
and in water.

Birds

Many water birds have webbed feet
to help them swim.
To help them float
their feathers are shiny with oil
which comes from a special gland.

Cormorant

Swan

Pochard

Coot

Moorhen

Grebe

Reed Bunting

Willow Tit

Heron

Sedge Warbler

Marsh Tit

Herons stand motionless waiting
for fish and other small animals
to come within reach.

Many other birds which cannot swim
live in the reeds and plants
beside the river.

37

Algae

The green scum which sometimes
appears on plants, stones
and the surface of still water
is *algae*.

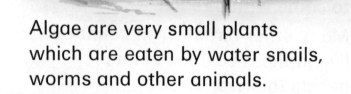

Algae are very small plants
which are eaten by water snails,
worms and other animals.

Insects and spiders

Water boatmen, pond skaters
and whirligig beetles
live on the surface of the water.

Wolf spiders and raft spiders
stay on top of the water.

The water spider
lives in an air bubble
under the water.

39

Freshwater Molluscs

Freshwater mussels and cockles
live in the mud and gravel.

Pollution

Dirty water from factories and towns
kills many plants and animals
in the river.

Both man and the creatures
that live in the river
need clean water.

Beside the river

Plants with tall stems
live at the water's edge.
Can you think why the flowers
are at the tops of the stems?

Reed

Yellow Flag

Meadowswe

Sed

Lesser Reedmace
(Bulrush)

Butter-bur

42

Flowers which like damp earth grow near the river.

Ragged Robin

Rushes

Fleabane

Meadow Rue

Lady's Smock

Marsh Marigold

Forget-me-not

43

The estuary

Where the river meets the sea
the water becomes salty.

The tide floods the estuary
and leaves marshes when it goes out.

Not many river plants and animals
can live here.

Rice Grass

Thrift

Marsh Samphire

Sea Aster

Around the estuary
land animals and plants
are found above the shoreline.

Gorse

Marram Grass

Sea Lavender

Sea Holly

Cup Lichen

Yellow Lichen

Sea Rocket

Scurvy Grass

Fish

Some fish such as minnows, roach and perch cannot live in salt water.

Salmon and sea trout spend part of their lives in the sea, but they have to lay their eggs in the fast flowing, fresh water of streams.

Salmon

Sea Trout

Marine molluscs

Some animals of the estuary
bury themselves
when the tide goes out.

Fishermen collect cockles with rakes.

Oysters and mussels cling to rocks
and stones.

Mussels

Dog Whelks

Edible Crab

Clam

Cockles

Periwinkles

Oysters

Birds

Sea birds such as
sea gulls and oystercatchers
search the muddy estuary for food.

They eat small fish,
molluscs (shellfish) and worms.

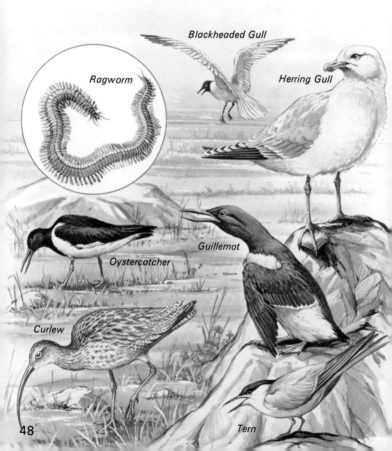

Ragworm

Blackheaded Gull

Herring Gull

Oystercatcher

Guillemot

Curlew

Tern

Seaweed

Seaweeds are algae.

Green seaweed can live
both in and out of water.

Brown seaweed lives in deeper water
and can only live out of water
for a short time.

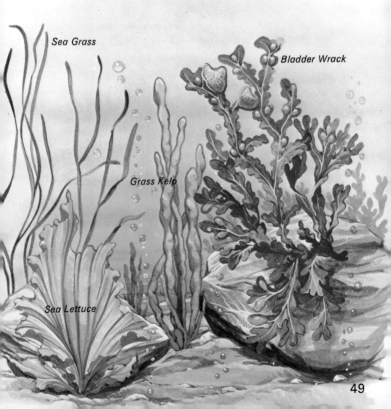

Sea Grass

Bladder Wrack

Grass Kelp

Sea Lettuce

The open coast

Where the mud changes to sand
very few plants grow,
except those that cling to rocks.

Everything that lives
on the open coast
has to be able to live
both in and out of the water.

Plants and animals are often hit
by waves and moving shingle.

Index